About Birds
Sobre los pájaros

A Guide for Children / Una guía para niños

Cathryn Sill

Illustrated by / *Ilustraciones de* John Sill

Translated by / *Traducción de* Cristina de la Torre

PEACHTREE

ATLANTA

For the One who created birds.
—Genesis 1:21

Para Aquél que creó a los pájaros.
—Génesis 1:21

Published by
PEACHTREE PUBLISHING COMPANY INC.
1700 Chattahoochee Avenue
Atlanta, Georgia 30318-2112
www.peachtreebooks.com

Text © 1991, 1997, 2013 by Cathryn P. Sill
Illustrations © 1991, 1997, 2013 by John C. Sill
Spanish translation © 2014 by Peachtree Publishers

First bilingual edition published in hardcover and trade paperback in 2014.

Also available in an English-language edition
HC ISBN: 978-1-56145-688-8
PB ISBN: 978-1-56145-699-4

The publisher thanks René Valdés for his guidance with the Spanish bird names.

Edited by Vicky Holifield
Spanish translation: Cristina de la Torre
Spanish-language copy editor: Cecilia Molinari

Illustrations painted in watercolor on archival quality 100% rag watercolor paper
Text and titles set in Novarese from Adobe Systems

Printed in October 2021 by Toppan Leefung in China

10 9 8 7 6 5 4 3 2 1 (bilingual hardcover)
10 9 8 7 6 5 (bilingual paperback)

HC ISBN: 978-1-56145-799-1
PB ISBN: 978-1-56145-783-0

Library of Congress Cataloging-in-Publication Data

Sill, Cathryn P., 1953— author.
About birds : a guide for children / Sobre los pájaros : una guía para niños / by Cathryn Sill ; illustrated by John Sill ; translated by Cristina de la Torre.
pages cm
ISBN: 978-1-56145-783-0
English and Spanish.
Includes bibliographical references and index.
1. Birds—Juvenile literature. I. Sill, John, illustrator. II. Sill, Cathryn P., 1953— About birds. III. Sill, Cathryn P., 1953— About birds. Spanish. IV. Title. V. Title: Sobre los pájaros.
QL676.2.S5318 2014
598—dc23
2013039824

About Birds

Sobre los pájaros

Birds have feathers.

Los pájaros tienen plumas.

PLATE 1 / LÁMINA 1
Northern Cardinal / *cardenal rojo*

Baby birds hatch from eggs.

Las crías de los pájaros salen de huevos.

PLATE 2 / LÁMINA 2
American Robin / *mirlo primavera*

John Gill

Some birds build nests on the ground.

Algunos pájaros hacen sus nidos en la tierra.

PLATE 3 / LÁMINA 3
Ovenbird / chipe suelero

Some build in very high places.

Algunos los hacen en lugares muy altos.

PLATE 4 / LÁMINA 4
Bald Eagle / *águila cabeza blanca*

And some do not build a nest at all.

Y otros no hacen nido alguno.

PLATE 5 / LÁMINA 5
Common Murre / *arao común*

Birds travel in different ways.

Los pájaros tienen distintos modos de viajar.

PLATE 6 / LÁMINA 6
Canada Goose / *ganso canadiense*

Most birds fly,

La mayoría de los pájaros vuela,

but some swim,

pero algunos nadan,

PLATE 8 / LÁMINA 8
Wood Duck / pato arcoíris

and others run.

y otros corren.

PLATE 9 / LÁMINA 9
Greater Roadrunner / *correcaminos norteñ*

Birds may flock together...

Los pájaros pueden formar bandadas...

or live alone.

o vivir solos.

PLATE 11 / LÁMINA 11
Great Horned Owl / *búho cornudo*

Birds use their bills to gather food.

Los pájaros usan el pico para recolectar alimentos.

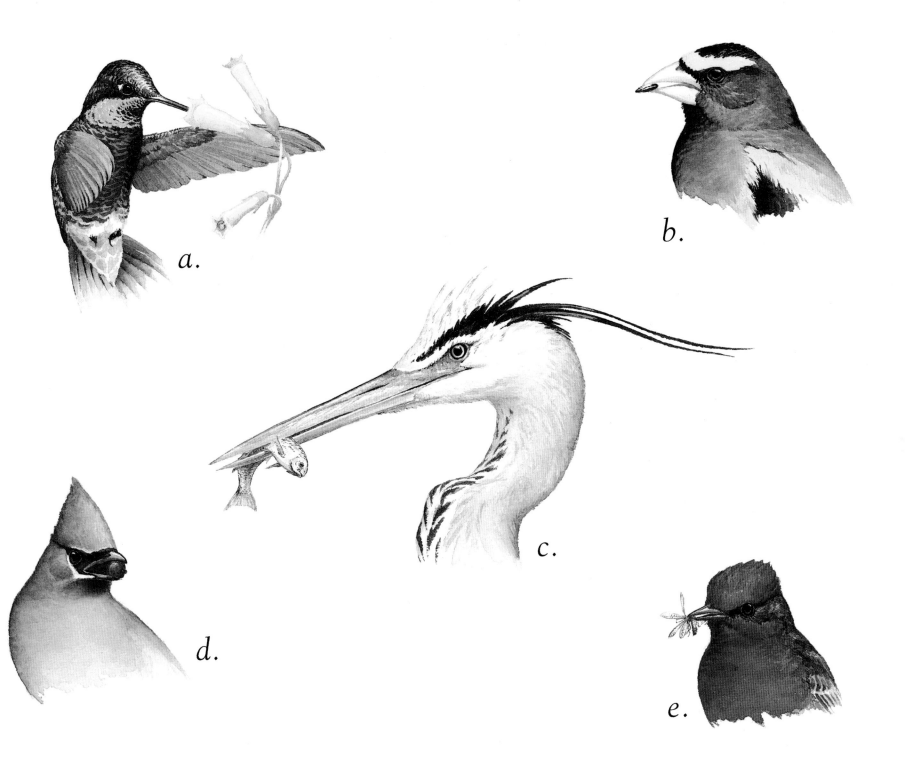

a.

b.

c.

d.

e.

They sing to let other birds know how they feel.

Cantan para que otros pájaros sepan cómo
se sienten.

PLATE 13 / LÁMINA 13
Indigo Bunting / *colorín azul*

Birds come in all sizes.

Hay pájaros de todos los tamaños.

Birds are important to us.

Los pájaros son importantes para nosotros.

PLATE 15 / LÁMINA 15
Common backyard birds of Eastern North America /
Pájaros comunes a los jardines del este de América del Norte

Afterword / Epílogo

PLATE 1

There are more than 10,000 species of birds in the world. Over 700 species live in the United States and Canada. Feathers protect birds from the elements. Because feathers are so light and strong, they enable birds to fly. Northern Cardinals are popular backyard birds in eastern areas of the U.S. and parts of the southwest. They live in brushy places with dense cover.

LÁMINA 1

Hay más de 10.000 especies de pájaros en el mundo. Más de 700 de ellas habitan en Estados Unidos y Canadá. Las plumas protegen a los pájaros de los elementos y, al ser fuertes y ligeras, posibilitan el vuelo. Los cardenales rojos son populares en los jardines del este de Estados Unidos y también en el suroeste del país. Viven entre densas malezas que los cubren.

PLATE 2

Although all birds hatch from eggs, different species have different nesting habits. Female American Robins build cup-shaped nests in shrubs or trees from materials such as twigs, grass, feathers, and string. The nest is reinforced with soft mud and lined with fine grasses. American Robins are common across North America in many habitats, including fields, forests, shrub lands, tundra, and yards.

LÁMINA 2

Aunque todos los pájaros salen de huevos sus nidos varían. Las hembras de los mirlos primavera hacen nidos en forma de cono en los arbustos o en los árboles usando ramitas, hierba, plumas y cuerda. Luego refuerzan el nido con fango y lo forran con hierba más fina. Los mirlos primavera son comunes en toda América del Norte en diversos hábitats, incluyendo campos, bosques, matorrales, tundra y jardines.

PLATE 3

Birds use nests to protect their eggs and chicks from predators and bad weather. Nests built on the ground are often hidden or camouflaged. Ovenbirds are named for their small dome-shaped nests that resemble old-fashioned ovens. These birds nest in forests across Canada and the eastern United States. In winter Ovenbirds migrate to the southeastern United States, the Caribbean, Mexico, Central America, and northern South America.

LÁMINA 3

Los pájaros hacen los nidos para proteger a sus huevos y crías de los depredadores y del mal tiempo. Los nidos construidos en la tierra a menudo están escondidos o camuflados. Los nidos de los chipes sueleros tienen forma de cúpula y se parecen a los hornos antiguos. Estos pájaros habitan los bosques de Canadá y del este de Estados Unidos. En invierno migran hacia el sudeste de Estados Unidos, el Caribe, México, América Central y el norte de América del Sur.

PLATE 4

Many birds build nests above the ground, varying the height according to the needs of individual species. Bald Eagles usually nest in tall trees that provide a wide view. They nest on cliff faces or even on the ground in areas where tall trees do not grow. Bald Eagles live in most of North America.

LÁMINA 4

Muchos pájaros construyen sus nidos en lo alto, variando la altura de acuerdo con las necesidades de las distintas especies. Las águilas cabeza blanca generalmente anidan en las copas de los árboles desde donde tienen un amplio panorama. En sitios donde no hay árboles altos, anidan en acantilados o a veces hasta en la tierra. Las águilas cabeza blanca se encuentran a lo largo y ancho de casi toda América del Norte.

PLATE 5

Some birds scrape out a place to lay eggs right on the ground. Common Murres lay pointed pear-shaped eggs on rocky ledges. The elongated shape of the eggs causes them to roll in a circular motion, thus preventing them from toppling off the edge. Common Murres live on northern oceans around the world. They only come to shore to nest.

LÁMINA 5

Algunos pájaros raspan el suelo para hacer un sitio donde poner sus huevos. Los araos comunes ponen sus huevos en forma de pera en cornisas rocosas. La forma alargada de los huevos hace que rueden en círculos y de ese modo no se caen de la cornisa. Los araos comunes viven en los mares del norte alrededor del mundo y solamente vienen a las zonas costeras para tener sus crías.

PLATE 6

Most birds use flight to move around. Flying helps them get food, find a safe place to raise young, and avoid predators. Canada Geese are strong flyers. They are able to migrate hundreds of miles in spring and fall. Canada Geese are native to most of North America. They have been introduced in England, northwest Europe, and New Zealand.

LÁMINA 6

La mayoría de los pájaros vuela para trasladarse. El vuelo les permite encontrar alimentos, lugares para criar a sus polluelos y evitar depredadores. Los gansos canadienses son magníficos voladores, capaces de desplazarse cientos de millas en sus migraciones de otoño y primavera. Los gansos canadienses son oriundos de casi toda América del Norte y han sido introducidos en Inglaterra, el noroeste de Europa y Nueva Zelanda.

PLATE 7

Hummingbirds are able to fly forward, backward, sideways, and upside down. Ruby-throated Hummingbirds are powerful fliers, beating their wings about 53 times per second. They nest in eastern North America and migrate to Central America for the winter. Many of them fly across the Gulf of Mexico in a single flight.

LÁMINA 7

Los colibríes pueden volar hacia delante, hacia atrás, hacia los lados y hasta patas arriba. Los colibríes garganta rubí son poderosos en el aire, capaces de batir las alas alrededor de 53 veces por segundo. Anidan en el este de América del Norte y migran hacia América Central durante el invierno. Muchos logran sobrevolar el Golfo de México de una sola vez.

PLATE 8

Some birds swim underwater to find food and avoid predators. Others stay on the surface most of the time. Wood Ducks have webbed feet that enable them to swim. They are also strong flyers. Wood Ducks live in wooded swamps and forested waterways across parts of North America and western Cuba.

LÁMINA 8

Algunos pájaros se sumergen en el agua en busca de alimentos y para escapar de sus depredadores. Otros se mantienen en la superficie casi todo el tiempo. Los patos arcoíris tienen patas palmeadas que les permiten nadar, aunque también son ágiles volando. Estos patos viven en pantanos boscosos y vías fluviales arboladas en partes de América del Norte y el oeste de Cuba.

PLATE 9

Birds that run spend much of their time on the ground. Most of them can also fly. Greater Roadrunners can run at speeds up to 18 mph (30 kph). They prefer running, but will fly to escape predators. Greater Roadrunners live in the southwestern United States and Mexico.

LÁMINA 9

Los pájaros corredores pasan gran parte del tiempo a ras del suelo. Muchos de ellos también vuelan. Los correcaminos norteños alcanzan velocidades de hasta 18 millas por hora (30 km). Prefieren correr, pero alzan vuelo para escapar de depredadores. Viven en zonas del suroeste de Estados Unidos y México.

PLATE 10

Some birds flock together in fall and winter for protection. Red-winged Blackbirds often form huge flocks made up of thousands of birds. During the nesting season the flocks separate and each pair claims its own territory. Red-winged Blackbirds live in North and Central America.

LÁMINA 10

Algunos pájaros se agrupan en bandadas en primavera y otoño para estar más protegidos. Las bandadas de tordos sargento a menudo cuentan con millares de ellos. En la época de apareamiento las bandadas se separan y cada pareja busca su propio territorio. Los tordos sargento habitan América del Norte y Central.

PLATE 11

Many birds of prey are solitary except during the nesting season. Great Horned Owls live in different habitats across most of North America. They also live in parts of Central and South America.

LÁMINA 11

Muchas aves de rapiña son solitarias excepto en temporada de apareamiento. Los búhos cornudos viven en diversos hábitats a lo largo y ancho de América del Norte así como en partes de América Central y del Sur.

PLATE 12

Birds' bills are shaped according to the food they eat. Birds also use their bills to preen their feathers, build nests, and defend themselves. Magnificent Hummingbirds live in the southwest United States and Central America. Evening Grosbeaks live in North America. Great Blue Herons and Cedar Waxwings live in North America, Central America, and northern parts of South America. Vermilion Flycatchers live in the southwestern United States, Central America, and South America.

LÁMINA 12

La forma de los picos de las aves la determinan los alimentos que consumen. Los pájaros también hacen uso del pico para limpiarse las plumas, hacer sus nidos y defenderse. Los colibríes magníficos viven en el suroeste de Estados Unidos y en América Central. Los picogruesos norteños viven en América del Norte. Las garzas morena y los ampelis chinito viven en América del Norte, América Central y zonas norteñas de América del Sur. Los mosqueros cardenales viven en el suroeste de Estados Unidos, América Central y América del Sur.

PLATE 13

Birds use their voices to attract mates, defend their territory, and warn others of danger. Indigo Buntings are small songbirds that spend the summer in eastern and central North America. They migrate to Central America and the West Indies for the winter.

LÁMINA 13

Los pájaros usan su canto para atraer pareja, defender su territorio y advertir a otros de peligro. Los colorines azules son pequeños pájaros cantores que pasan el verano en partes del este y centro de América del Norte. En invierno migran a América Central y a las islas de las Antillas y las Bahamas.

PLATE 14

Sizes of the illustrated birds:
a. Great Blue Heron—length 38" (96 cm), wingspan 70" (177 cm)
b. Bald Eagle—length 32" (81 cm), wingspan 80" (203 cm)
c. Great Horned Owl—length 20" (50 cm), wingspan 55" (139 cm)
d. Canada Goose—length 21½–43" (55–110 cm), wingspan 48–71½" (122–183 cm)
e. Wood Duck—length 13½" (34 cm), wingspan 28" (71 cm)
f. Northern Cardinal—length 7¾" (19.6 cm)
g. Red-winged Blackbird—length 7¼" (18 cm)
h. Indigo Bunting—length 4½" (11½ cm)
i. Ruby-throated Hummingbird—length 3¾" (9½ cm)

LÁMINA 14

Tamaño de los pájaros en las ilustraciones:
a. garza morena: largo 38" (96 cm), envergadura 70" (177 cm)
b. águila cabeza blanca: largo 32" (81 cm), envergadura 80" (203 cm)
c. búho cornudo: largo 20" (50 cm), envergadura 55" (139 cm)
d. ganso canadiense: largo 21½–43" (55–110 cm), envergadura 48–71½" (122–183 cm)
e. pato arcoíris: largo 13½" (34 cm), envergadura 28" (71 cm)
f. cardenal rojo: largo 7¾" (19,6 cm)
g. tordo sargento: largo 7¼" (18 cm)
h. colorín azul: largo 4½" (11½ cm)
i. colibrí garganta rubí: largo 3¾" (9½ cm)

PLATE 15

Birds benefit human beings in many ways. They eat harmful insects, pollinate some flowers, disperse seeds, keep rodent populations down, and provide food for people. Observing birds brings great pleasure to people all over the world.

LÁMINA 15

Los pájaros benefician a los seres humanos de diversos modos: comen insectos dañinos, polinizan algunas flores, esparcen las semillas, controlan el número de roedores y proveen alimentos para las personas. Observar a los pájaros es un gran placer para gente de todo el mundo.

GLOSSARY

Camouflage—colors or patterns on an animal that help it hide
Migrate—to move periodically from one region to another
Predator—an animal that lives by hunting and eating other animals
Preen—to straighten or clean feathers
Species—a group of animals or plants that are alike in many ways

GLOSARIO

Camuflaje: colores o diseños en los animales que ayudan a esconderlos.
Migrar: cambiar periódicamente de una región a otra.
Depredador: un animal que sobrevive cazando y alimentándose de otros animales.
Especie: grupos de animales o plantas que son similares en muchos aspectos.

BIBLIOGRAPHY

BOOKS

BIRD (DK Eyewitness Books)
A PLACE FOR BIRDS by Melissa Stewart (Peachtree Publishers)
NATIONAL AUDUBON SOCIETY FIRST FIELD GUIDE: BIRDS by Scott Weidensaul (Scholastic, Inc.)
PETERSON FIRST GUIDES: BIRDS by Roger Tory Peterson (Houghton Mifflin Company)
THE YOUNG BIRDERS GUIDE TO BIRDS OF EASTERN NORTH AMERICA by Bill Thompson III (Houghton Mifflin Company)

WEBSITES

http://www.allaboutbirds.org/guide/search/ac
http://ibc.lynxeds.com/
http://animaldiversity.ummz.umich.edu./site/accounts/information/Aves.html

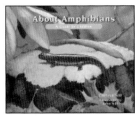

About Amphibians
A Guide for Children

HC: 978-1-68263-031-0
PB: 978-1-68263-032-7

About Arachnids
A Guide for Children

HC: 978-1-56145-038-1
PB: 978-1-56145-364-1

About Birds
A Guide for Children

HC: 978-1-56145-688-8
PB: 978-1-56145-699-4

About Crustaceans
A Guide for Children

HC: 978-1-56145-301-6
PB: 978-1-56145-405-1

About Fish
A Guide for Children

HC: 978-1-56145-987-2
PB: 978-1-56145-988-9

About Hummingbirds
A Guide for Children

HC: 978-1-56145-588-1
PB: 978-1-56145-837-0

About Insects
A Guide for Children

HC: 978-1-56145-881-3
PB: 978-1-56145-882-0

About Mammals
A Guide for Children

HC: 978-1-56145-757-1
PB: 978-1-56145-758-8

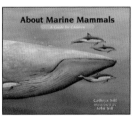

About Marine Mammals
A Guide for Children

HC: 978-1-56145-906-3

About Marsupials
A Guide for Children

HC: 978-1-56145-358-0
PB: 978-1-56145-407-5

About Mollusks
A Guide for Children

PB: 978-1-56145-406-8

About Parrots
A Guide for Children

HC: 978-1-56145-795-3

About Penguins
A Guide for Children

HC: 978-1-56145-743-4
PB: 978-1-56145-741-0

About Raptors
A Guide for Children

HC: 978-1-56145-536-2
PB: 978-1-56145-811-0

About Reptiles
A Guide for Children

HC: 978-1-56145-907-0
PB: 978-1-56145-908-7

About Rodents
A Guide for Children

HC: 978-1-56145-454-9
PB: 978-1-56145-914-8

About Woodpeckers
A Guide for Children

HC: 978-1-68263-004-4

ALSO AVAILABLE IN SPANISH AND BILINGUAL EDITIONS

- About Amphibians / Sobre los anfibios / 978-1-68263-033-4 PB ● About Birds / Sobre los pájaros / 978-1-56145-783-0 PB ● Sobre los pájaros / 978-1-68263-071-6 PB
- About Fish / Sobre los peces / 978-1-56145-989-6 PB ● About Insects / Sobre los insectos / 978-1-56145-883-7 PB ● About Mammals / Sobre los mamíferos / 978-1-56145-800-4 PB ● Sobre los mamíferos / 978-1-68263-072-3 PB ● About Reptiles / Sobre los reptiles / 978-1-56145-909-4 PB

John Sill

ABOUT HABITATS SERIES

HC: 978-1-56145-641-3
PB: 978-1-56145-636-9

HC: 978-1-56145-734-2

HC: 978-1-56145-559-1
PB: 978-1-68263-034-1

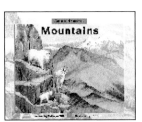

HC: 978-1-56145-469-3
PB: 978-1-56145-731-1

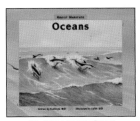

HC: 978-1-56145-618-5
PB: 978-1-56145-960-5

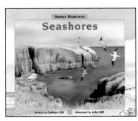

HC: 978-1-56145-832-5

HC: 978-1-56145-968-1

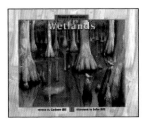

HC: 978-1-56145-432-7
PB: 978-1-56145-689-5

THE SILLS

Cathryn Sill, a graduate of Western Carolina University, was an elementary school teacher for thirty years.

John Sill is a prize-winning and widely published wildlife artist. A native of North Carolina, he holds a B.S. in wildlife biology from North Carolina State University.

The Sills have published eighteen books about nature for children. They live in North Carolina.

Cathryn Sill, graduada de Western Carolina University, fue maestra de escuela primaria durante treinta años.

John Sill es un pintor de vida silvestre que ha publicado ampliamente y merecido diversos galardones. Nacido en Carolina del Norte, es diplomado en biología de vida silvestre por North Carolina State University.

Los Sill, que han colaborado en dieciocho libros sobre la naturaleza para niños, viven en Carolina del Norte.